Tom on the Team

Mary O'Keeffe

Mr Lillis was the best teacher ever.

He liked to get out and about with the class.

Tom and Peter wanted to be just like him.

They liked to play all kinds of sports when they could.

One Tuesday, Mr Lillis had big news!

Next term, there would be a **hurling team** in the school!

"Tom, if we try out, we could join the **team**!" said Peter.

Try-outs were due to be held after school.

"We're fit, Peter, so you should have no **jitters**!" said Tom.

Tom went to join the queue to put on his kit.

He had his kit bag under his arm.

He put his blue top on **over** his vest.

Next, he put on his socks.

Then, Tom looked for his boots.

He got the right one out of his bag.

Then he got the next one out.

Hang on! There were two right boots in his bag!

And two left!

Oh no! Meg and Mel must have had the bag last!

"You can't try out today, Tom," said Mr Lillis in a stern voice.

"Don't argue. There's just no point."

Tom kicked at the soil.

"Oh Tom! You will get **over** it," said Peter.

Tom did not want to ever get **over** it.

He wanted to join the **team**.

"Could we go to the **sports shop**?" asked Tom. "I should have a kit bag of my own."

"That's true," said Dad. "Let's all go!"

There were lots of offers in the **sports shop**.

Tom found a kit bag in the right colours.

"Watch out!" said Dad. "Mr Lillis could want a loan of that!"

"We're due some new runners too!" said Meg and Mel with a pout.

"Let's avoid a row," said Mam. "These are two for the cost of one!"

After that, Tom put all of his kit into his new kit bag.

Two boots… one left and one right!

He would be ready for the next round of try-outs!

The next Tuesday, Tom put on his kit.

"No **jitters**!" said Peter with a grin. "Have some water before you go out onto the sports ground."

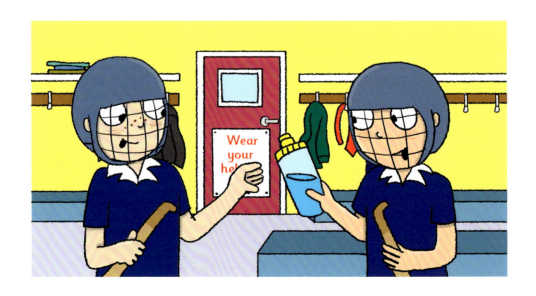

Tom went out.

He got his **hurley** and tossed the **sliotar** up off the ground.

Wow! It went **over** the bar!

What a point!

"Super, Tom!" said Mr Lillis with a loud shout. "You can join the **team**!"

Peter gave Tom a fist bump.

"With you on our **team**, we're bound to be even better!" he said.